50 Quick a...'s

Leade... ...are

for ...sted

By Mike Gershon

About the Author

Mike Gershon is a teacher, trainer and writer. He is the author of twenty books on teaching, learning and education, including a number of bestsellers, as well as the co-author of one other. Mike's online resources have been viewed and downloaded more than 2.5 million times by teachers in over 180 countries and territories. He is a regular contributor to the Times Educational Supplement and has created a series of electronic CPD guides for TES PRO. Find out more, get in touch and download free resources at www.mikegershon.com

Training and Consultancy

Mike is an expert trainer whose sessions have received acclaim from teachers across England. Recent bookings include:

- *Improving Literacy Levels in Every Classroom*, St Leonard's Academy, Sussex

- *Growth Mindsets, Effective Marking and Feedback* Ash Manor School, Aldershot

- *Effective Differentiation,* Tri-Borough Alternative Provision (TBAP), London

Mike also works as a consultant, advising on teaching and learning and creating bespoke materials for schools. Recent work includes:

- *Developing and Facilitating Independent Learning,* Chipping Norton School, Oxfordshire

- *Differentiation In-Service Training,* Charles Darwin School, Kent

If you would like speak to Mike about the services he can offer your school, please get in touch by email: mike@mikegershon.com

Other Works from the Same Authors

Available to buy now on Amazon:

How to use Differentiation in the Classroom: The Complete Guide

How to use Assessment for Learning in the Classroom: The Complete Guide

How to use Questioning in the Classroom: The Complete Guide

How to use Discussion in the Classroom: The Complete Guide

How to Teach EAL Students in the Classroom: The Complete Guide

More Secondary Starters and Plenaries

Secondary Starters and Plenaries: History

Teach Now! History: Becoming a Great History Teacher

The Growth Mindset Pocketbook (with Professor Barry Hymer)

How to be Outstanding in the Classroom

Also available to buy now on Amazon, the entire 'Quick 50' Series:

50 Quick and Brilliant Teaching Ideas

50 Quick and Brilliant Teaching Techniques

50 Quick and Easy Lesson Activities

50 Quick Ways to Help Your Students Secure A and B Grades at GCSE

50 Quick Ways to Help Your Students Think, Learn, and Use Their Brains Brilliantly

50 Quick Ways to Motivate and Engage Your Students

50 Quick Ways to Outstanding Teaching

50 Quick Ways to Perfect Behaviour Management

50 Quick and Brilliant Teaching Games

50 Quick and Easy Ways to Outstanding Group Work

50 Quick and Easy Ways to Prepare for Ofsted

50 Quick and Easy Ways Leaders can Prepare for Ofsted

About the Series

The 'Quick 50' series was born out of a desire to provide teachers with practical, tried and tested ideas, activities, strategies and techniques which would help them to teach brilliant lessons, raise achievement and engage and inspire their students.

Every title in the series distils great teaching wisdom into fifty bite-sized chunks. These are easy to digest and easy to apply – perfect for the busy teacher who wants to develop their practice and support their students.

Acknowledgements

As ever I must thank all the fantastic colleagues and students I have worked with over the years, first while training at the Institute of Education, Central Foundation Girls' School and Nower Hill High School and subsequently while working at Pimlico Academy and King Edward VI School in Bury St Edmunds.

Thanks also to Alison and Andrew Metcalfe for a great place to write and finally to Gordon at KallKwik for help with the covers.

Table of Contents

Introduction

Know Your Priorities Inside Out

Why are they your priorities?

What is being done about them?

How are you contributing to meeting the priorities?

How will the school assess whether it has achieved its priorities?

Know the Data!

Ensure There is a Clear Narrative Around the Data

Do Not Allow For Any Surprises

Show Clearly How Data is Being Used

Look at Data in the Context of Progress

Look at Data in the Context of Specific Groups

Check Marking

Is there a marking policy (or marking guidance)?

Formative, Target-Driven, Positive Marking

Do Your Own Marking

Work Scrutiny

Students who are on the SEN Register

Pupil Premium Students

Students who have free school meals

Students for who English is an additional language

Students who are gifted and talented

Familiarise Yourself with the Relevant Documentation

Examine Good Practice Guides

Identify what is Expected of Leaders

Share Relevant Documents with Colleagues

Speak to Colleagues in Other Schools

What is your role and why does it exist?

What do you do and how does it contribute to the school?

What impact do you have on colleagues and students?

How are you supporting the school's priorities?

How are you supporting the colleagues you manage?

Familiarise Yourself with the Process

Speak to colleagues who have been through the process

Rehearse

Mock Ofsted

Communicate to Colleagues

Identify who you need to support and support them

Share Your Expertise

Share any Knowledge you Accrue

Let people know clearly and explicitly what is required of them

Make sure people look after themselves

Don't Let it Become a Behemoth

Analyse Your School in Accordance with the Reporting System

Identify Areas for Immediate Intervention

Find Positive Solutions

Avoid Blame and Recrimination

Evaluate the Strengths and Weaknesses of the School

Be Ready to Play Up the Strengths

Be ready to explain the weaknesses and how you are responding

Show Pride in the Things You Do Really Well

A Brief Request

Introduction

Welcome to '50 Quick and Easy Ways Leaders can Prepare for Ofsted.'

This book is all about the things you as a leader can do to prepare for an Ofsted inspection. It provides practical advice, strategies and ideas you can implement to support others, ensure your school is well-set for any inspection and be certain that you are doing the best job possible.

Of course, the results of an inspection depend on the judgements the inspectors make. This book makes no claims that it will help you to achieve a specific grade.

What it does offer though, is suggestions on how to prepare, the kind of things which you need to think about and the various resources which are out there waiting to be used.

The focus is practical throughout. Every entry offers something tangible which you can do or use to help prepare yourself, your colleagues and your school.

And the overall aim is simple: to help you to prepare as effectively as possible for any upcoming visits you might have from Ofsted.

So read on and enjoy; and if you do get inspected, good luck!

Know Your Priorities Inside Out

01 Your priorities define what you as a school are trying to do to raise achievement, secure improvement and generally move things on from where they currently are.

As a leader, one of your responsibilities is to contribute to the school achieving its goals. The specific nature of your role will determine the level to which you can contribute. But, of course, we can all contribute to some extent.

If you don't know the school's priorities, find out what they are.

When you know the priorities, interrogate them. Make sure you can talk expertly about them and connect them to your own role.

If your role has other priorities outside of the whole-school ones, be certain to make sure you know these inside out as well.

The aim, as in any situation where you might be asked questions, is to ensure that you are knowledgeable, confident and have the relevant information to hand.

Why are they your priorities?

02 When thinking and talking about the school's priorities with colleagues, ensure you and they know why they are your priorities. This is a very reasonable question you could be asked. Life will be much easier if you have analysed and then rehearsed the answer in advance.

For example, one of your priorities might be to raise the achievement of white working-class boys. The reason for this may be that the data has shown a large gap between their achievement and overall results. As a school you know it is your duty to try to secure the best outcomes for all students. Therefore you are putting things in place to improve the situation.

It might be that you have multiple priorities and, due to having limited resources, certain ones have been put to the top of the list. If this is so, make sure you know why that decision has been made. What criteria have been used to make the judgement?

What is being done about them?

03 As a leader you are part of the school's management structure. This could be the middle-management or the senior management. Either way, it is important that you know what the school is doing to try to meet its goals.

The reasons are threefold.

First, it illustrates a high level of professionalism, demonstrating that you are knowledgeable and informed about the position of the school, where it is heading and how it is going to get there.

Second, it means you can assess how you are contributing to achieving the goals and how individuals and/or departments you lead or manage are contributing.

Third, good leadership is proactive. If you know what is being done, why it is being done and what the intended results are, you are being proactive. Furthermore, so is your school. This will reflect well on you.

How are you contributing to meeting the priorities?

04 We have touched on this in the first three entries.

Leaders lead. They take others forward, through example, support, teaching, decision-making and so on. Leaders have responsibilities – to the school, to colleagues, to students, to governors and to parents.

Central to these responsibilities is trying to improve things. Therefore, it is important that you assess how you are contributing to the school's priorities. Ideally, you want to be in a position where you can communicate this clearly should anyone ask. It will be even better if you can provide evidence which supports the claims you make.

It is also worth assessing how those people you lead and manage are contributing to the priorities. Again, you want to be in a position from where you can talk confidently and openly about this.

How will the school assess whether it has achieved its priorities?

05 When we try to achieve something we need to understand what that achievement is going to be judged against.

If we do not know this, we will never know if we have achieved anything. For example, if I run in a race, I might judge my achievement against the clock. Or, I might judge it against who I beat.

If you do not know how your school will assess whether or not it has achieved its priorities then you are, to some extent, throwing sand into the wind. Who knows where it will go? And who will have any means to judge whether this was intended or not.

Find out how the school will assess its attempts to achieve its priorities. Learn this and then be ready to talk about it with confidence and precision.

Know the Data!

06 Data is central to the inspection process. It provides a clear sense of what is happening in your school in terms of achievement and how this is playing out historically (through year-on-year analysis, the identification of trends and historical comparisons).

Ofsted provide two useful online data services you can use to find out information about individual schools and wider regions:

- Ofsted Data View

- School Data Dashboard

It is vital that you know your school's data and what this means. Furthermore, if you are responsible for a department or a series of departments, you should know their data as well.

Put simply, this is about you having the information about achievement at your fingertips. After all, this is the information which illustrates how the school is performing, what outcomes are being delivered for pupils and what needs to be done to improve.

Ensure There is a Clear Narrative Around the Data

07 By this we mean that data on its own is just numbers. A clear narrative contextualises data and ties it into the things which are actually taking place in your school (the data is not a thing in itself, remember. It is a numerical representation of what has happened).

So, for example, if you have seen achievement dip and you have worked quickly to address this, explain the data in terms of this narrative. In so doing you will be illustrating that you are using the data in order to make sound decisions about the needs of students and the school.

If you can't explain the data, this will reflect poorly. Because, as we mentioned, the data is a clear, statistical indication of what is happening in the school in terms of outcomes and achievement.

Do Not Allow For Any Surprises

08 This is difficult to fully achieve because surprises, by their nature, may not all be spottable.

However, in every walk of life, the best way to avoid surprises is by being thorough, methodical, organised and well-prepared.

You can do this by:

- Familiarising yourself with the inspection process

- Analysing the data in detail

- Rehearsing how you would answer different questions put to you by the inspection team

- Conducting a mock inspection (or individual elements thereof)

- Walking through the different aspects of the school, the data, your priorities and so forth

This may take a little bit of time but the benefits will not be restricted to the inspection itself. Everything you find out can be used to aid the school and your students in general. Therefore, the processes through which you minimise the chance of any surprises arising will also improve your ability to do your job well and contribute to the school's success.

Show Clearly How Data is Being Used

09 As we have noted, data is a tool. In fact, it is one of the most useful tools available to any school. Data illustrates what is happening in terms of learning and outcomes. It provides a detailed picture of the progress pupils are making and the results they are achieving.

Data can be used in myriad ways. Some of these include:

- Tracking individual students

- Establishing which pupils need extra support or intervention

- Monitoring the achievement levels of different groups

- Assessing whether teaching and learning strategies have their desired effect

- Making comparisons between different groups, years and subjects

In every case, the data is being used. It has a purpose. And that purpose links to the school's overall aim: raising achievement and securing superb outcomes.

Being able to show clearly how data is being used means you will be able to show clearly how you and the school are responding proactively to the information you have about achievement and progress.

Look at Data in the Context of Progress

10 One of the key ways in which you can look at data is in the context of progress. By progress we really mean learning that is visible and recordable through assessment.

Using the lens of progress you can analyse your school's data in search of trends and patterns which show the kind of outcomes that pupils are achieving. You can then use this information in ways such as those outlined in entry nine.

Thinking about data in the context of progress is a quick way to cut through what might initially feel overwhelming. Not everyone is at ease with numbers. And even those who are can struggle to see the wood for the trees if there is a very large amount of data to wade through. Thinking in terms of progress allows you to focus on what matters.

Look at Data in the Context of Specific Groups

11 Specific groups are another lens through which you can analyse your data. Groups include:

- SEN students

- EAL students

- FSM students

- Pupil Premium students

- G and T Students

- Students categorised according to ethnicity, class, gender or a combination of these

In all cases, the purpose is to compare the outcomes these groups are securing with overall outcomes and with outcomes different groups are securing. These comparisons will allow you to identify if interventions or changes need to be made.

Looking at your data in the context of specific groups will also indicate that you are proactively responding to the challenges all schools face: namely, ensuring every pupil, regardless of background or starting point, makes outstanding progress.

Check Marking

12 Marking is an essential part of ensuring progress. Various studies (Black et al 2003; Hattie 2012) have indicated that high-quality feedback has a significant impact on student achievement.

Its effects are right up at the top of the scale.

Of course, this is logically deducible:

- If pupils are to improve, they need to know what to do.

- Teachers know what pupils need to do to improve.

- Teachers can tell and show pupils what they need to do by marking their work.

- Pupils will then be in a position to improve.

You should check the marking teachers are doing in your school. Look at books, talk to colleagues, find examples of best practice and share these.

Inspectors will look at pupils' books. They will want to see evidence of high-quality marking and feedback. Get in there first to make sure it is happening.

Is there a marking policy (or marking guidance)?

13 A marking policy, or marking guidance, tells teachers and students across the school what is to be expected. This is the beauty of policies, they formalise behaviour across an institution, to the intended benefit of all.

Rigid policies can stifle innovation so you do need to be thoughtful when implementing them. However, given what we know about effective marking (formative, providing guidance on how to improve, grades kept separate from comments – see the research noted in the previous entry) and its importance, it seems reasonable to assume that a marking policy ought to be in place.

If you do have one, make sure everyone is familiar with it. If you don't have one, ask why. There may be a very good reason but it will look much better if you know this in advance (rather than finding yourself caught out).

Formative, Target-Driven, Positive Marking

14 As mentioned in the previous entry, research suggests pretty clear things about marking.

First, it should be formative. That is, developmental. Formative comments tell students what they need to do to improve and how to do it. They also indicate what has been done well and why.

Second, formative feedback should contain a clear target that students can work to implement. This is the crux of how they will improve, based on the teacher's feedback.

Third, marking should be positive. For example, teachers can give three strengths and one area for improvement, or they can use the pupil's name when they write their target. Positive interactions of any form are more likely to engage and motivate than the converse.

You can use all this information to communicate to colleagues what great marking should look like and why this will lead to significant progress.

Do Your Own Marking

15 And don't forget to do your own marking! As a school leader, you will likely have a lot on your plate. However, if you still teach lessons then you still need to do your marking.

What with everything else you'll be doing and thinking about, this can easily be forgotten. So make a point of getting on top of it. After all, your pupils need your feedback if they are to make the best progress possible.

Work Scrutiny

16 Work scrutiny involves middle and senior leaders taking samples of books in order to gain an understanding of what is going on in lessons, how pupils are working, the kind of progress which is happening, and the type and quality of marking which is taking place.

Work scrutiny can be done on a department-by-department basis, it can focus on specific groups of students, or it can be conducted using a random sampling method.

However you do it, the purpose is to elicit information which you as a leader can use. If things look great, fantastic. Having evidence to support this judgement is good.

If you uncover problems, equally brilliant. You can now focus on remedying the situation by supporting students and colleagues to secure improvements.

Whatever the results of work scrutiny, you will have more information about what is happening in the school and how you can help others to improve.

Students who are on the SEN Register

17 Let us now spend five entries focussing on different groups of students and thinking about how you as a leader can support them and support the teachers who work with them.

Every school should have an SEN register managed by its SENCO. This register sets out which pupils have special educational needs, what these needs are, what support is being given and any special points of which staff need to be aware.

Here are five ways in which you can support colleagues in terms of SEN students:

- Make sure they know where the register is and how to access it.

- If you are the SENCO, ensure the register is up-to-date and actively promote it to colleagues.

- Share good practice on working with SEN students during briefings, via email or in newsletters.

- Remind colleagues to differentiate for SEN pupils. Provide or collate practical examples of how to do this.

- Analyse the school's data to assess whether or not SEN students are making good progress. If they are not, look at how you and the leadership team can improve matters.

Pupil Premium Students

18 Pupil premium students are students from a disadvantaged background who attract an additional payment from the government. This policy was introduced by the coalition and is aimed at improving the life-chances of these pupils.

In short, it is expected that the money will be used to help these students succeed.

Ideally, your school should have a register of pupil premium students. Staff should know who these pupils are and, where possible, should be differentiating to help them succeed.

In addition, there should be a clear indication of how the pupil premium money is being spent and what impact this is having on the students in question. One common use is to fund intervention tutors who can work intensively with these pupils on literacy and numeracy.

For information from the government about the pupil premium, visit https://www.gov.uk/government/policies/raising-the-achievement-of-disadvantaged-children/supporting-pages/pupil-premium.

For an excellent toolkit on how to use the Pupil Premium effectively (created by the Education Endowment Foundation), visit http://educationendowmentfoundation.org.uk/toolkit/.

Students who have free school meals

19 Free school meals are traditionally used as an indicator of economic disadvantage, for obvious reasons. Students who receive free school meals can be identified as having a lower socio-economic status than their peers. Of course, this is not always true (some parents may not apply for free school meals because they feel a stigma is attached to them), but the measure is still a useful one to use.

You should analyse the school's data to assess whether or not FSM students are achieving outcomes comparable to their peers. If they are not, you and the leadership team need to intervene.

Here is a useful document which can help you to raise achievement:

http://www.c4eo.org.uk/themes/schools/classrooms trategies/files/classroom_strategies_research_revie w.pdf (Research review into effective classroom strategies for closing the gap in educational achievement).

Students for who English is an additional language

20 The percentage of students for who English is an additional language varies considerably across the country. These pupils are another group whose progress you need to assess in comparison to the overall progress of students in your school.

Again, the intention is to identify whether EAL pupils are making the progress we would want them to make. If they are not, you can use the information you have elicited from the data to develop positive and helpful interventions.

For advice and guidance on teaching and supporting EAL students, see http://www.naldic.org.uk/. This is the website of the National Association for Language Development in the Curriculum.

You might also like to take a look at my free resource The EAL Toolkit and my book How to Teach EAL Students in the Classroom: The Complete Guide.

Students who are gifted and talented

21 The final group of students of whom we must take note are those designated as gifted and talented. Ideally, your school will have a register of who these students are and one or more members of staff will have responsibility for ensuring good quality G and T provision across the school.

As with each of the groups we have looked at, you can analyse your school's assessment data to ascertain whether or not G and T pupils are achieving the outcomes you would expect.

To help staff with stretching and challenging gifted and talented students, you might like to point them in the direction of my free resource, The Challenge Toolkit.

Another good resource is the London Gifted & Talented website. You can find it at http://teachertools.londongt.org/.

Familiarise Yourself with the Relevant Documentation

22 Having considered the different groups of students you as a leader need to be aware of let us now go on to look at documentation and the Ofsted website.

The first and most obvious point is that, when preparing for an inspection, you should familiarise yourself with the relevant documentation.

You can find it here:
http://www.ofsted.gov.uk/schools/for-schools/inspecting-schools

Specifically:

- The framework for school inspection

- What happens before, during and after an inspection

- Main inspection documents for inspectors

You might also like to look at the frequently asked questions guidance which you can access at
https://www.gov.uk/government/collections/ofsteds-inspection-of-schools

(all links accessed April 2014).

Examine Good Practice Guides

23 A little known fact about the Ofsted website is that it contains a large collection of good practice guides. You can find these here:

http://www.ofsted.gov.uk/resources/goodpractice

Simply use the search options to find the type of resource you want.

There is a wealth of information here. See what you can find and identify how you might apply it to your school.

Identify what is Expected of Leaders

24 As a leader you make a specific and defined contribution to the effectiveness of your school. The overall effectiveness of leadership and management is judged during an inspection.

At present (April 2014) the five judgements Ofsted make are:

- Overall Effectiveness

- Achievement of Pupils

- Quality of Teaching

- Behaviour and Safety of Pupils

- Leadership and Management

You contribute to all of these as part of your role.

In consideration of the last one, leadership and management, you can find information about what inspectors will judge on pages 19 and 20 of the framework for school inspection (points 58 – 60).

Information on what inspectors will look at for the other parts can be found on pages 17-19 of the same document (points 48-57).

Share Relevant Documents with Colleagues

25 Once you have accessed and assimilated the relevant documents as part of your preparation, share them with your colleagues.

This will help everybody in the school understand what the inspection is about, what it will focus on, how judgements will be made and what can be done to create the best impression possible.

Knowledge is power. Knowledge allows you to make sound decisions and act well. Sharing knowledge with colleagues is therefore a powerful thing you can do as a leader.

Speak to Colleagues in Other Schools

26 Speaking of knowledge, another way in which you can find out about the process of an inspection is by talking to any colleagues you know in other schools where an inspection has recently taken place.

A few caveats however.

First, make sure you know if any aspect of the inspection process has changed since your colleagues were inspected. You don't want to be working under incorrect assumptions.

Second, don't assume that the same inspection team will inspect your school just because you are nearby. You may well get a completely different team of inspectors.

Third, treat the information you glean like you would any other – critically, carefully and with cross-reference to other sources.

What is your role and why does it exist?

27 We move now to look at some questions you can ask yourself to ensure you are personally prepared to speak confidently and coherently about your role.

The central point here is that preparation and rehearsal will make it easier for you to do yourself justice when the inspection team come into school. (It will also help you more widely as it will give you a greater sense of clarity concerning your work as a leader).

So, ask yourself this question: What is my role and why does it exist? I'm sure the answer will be pretty straightforward! Nonetheless, we all know how easy it is to lose the underlying simplicity of things amid the hustle and bustle of school life.

When you have your answer, you can use this as a guiding light for what you do and the professional decisions you make. It will act as a lens through which you can make sound judgements.

What do you do and how does it contribute to the school?

28 Next, ask yourself this question:

What do I do and how does it contribute to the school?

Think about it in detail. I am frequently staggered by the discrepancy between what teachers think they contribute and what they actually do contribute. They usually do **a lot more** than they realise!

Making clear in your mind how you contribute – even going so far as to make a bullet point list – will make it easier for you to talk about this to an inspector.

It will also help you to stay positive in times of stress because you can remind yourself that every day you are doing things which make a tangible difference to the school's success and, by extension, the achievement of your students.

What impact do you have on colleagues and students?

29 Now is the time to get a little more specific, so ask yourself:

What impact do I have on colleagues and students?

As a leader, I'm sure you will make a big impact. The important thing here is to know in advance what this impact is so that you can talk about it with confidence and authority.

You might also like to ask yourself a sub-question, namely:

What evidence is there of my impact?

Evidence is proof supporting the validity of a statement. We can all say things. Whether they are true or not is a different matter. Evidence is the means by which we ascertain proof in our society. If proof is not forthcoming, we tend to doubt the veracity of the statement (unless we are misled by other means such as charisma or rhetoric).

How are you supporting the school's priorities?

30 Two final questions now, the first of which is:

What am I doing to support the school's priorities?

We talked about the importance of the school's priorities in entries one to five and this is really just a reminder that, in the midst of clarifying your contribution to leadership and management, you should make sure you know precisely how you are supporting the priorities.

As mentioned previously, it is always preferable to support a claim with evidence. So if you can identify evidence which shows how you are supporting the priorities, all the better.

How are you supporting the colleagues you manage?

31 Our final question to ask is:

How am I supporting the colleagues I manage?

A supplement to this is:

How am I supporting the colleagues I lead?

Remember that leadership and management are two different things, though they are often intertwined. You might like to think of management as piloting the aircraft and leadership as plotting the route.

Again, having the answer to this question clear in your own mind will make it easier for you to talk confidently and coherently about your role.

Familiarise Yourself with the Process

32 In any situation that is important to us, it is to our benefit if we familiarise ourselves with what is likely to happen. This is for three reasons.

First, it minimises the likelihood that we will find ourselves shocked or surprised.

Second, it allows us to devote our full attention to the situation itself, when it arrives (we don't need to split our attention because we already know what to expect).

Third, we are able to plan more accurately and appropriately than would otherwise be the case.

In short, familiarising yourself with the inspection process will put you at your ease and help you to prepare more effectively than would otherwise be the case.

Speak to colleagues who have been through the process

33 As we mentioned in entry twenty-six, speaking to colleagues in other schools can be helpful. This is also true when we are looking to familiarise ourselves with the inspection process. The same caveats apply as were mentioned previously.

There are three other sources of information you might tap in a similar vein:

- Colleagues in your own school who have been through a recent inspection.

- Colleagues at the local authority or within your academy chain who have recently been through an inspection.

- Colleagues or former colleagues who work as inspectors and who might be able to provide guidance on how the process plays out.

With all that said, the Ofsted website will still be your main point of call for information on how the process works.

Rehearse

34 Rehearsals are practice. Practice allows us to improve. We improve by making mistakes and learning from them, by refining and clarifying, and by becoming increasingly familiar with the thing we are trying to do.

You can practice the following:

- Teaching outstanding lessons (which I'm sure you do every day).

- Facilitating outstanding progress (ditto).

- Explaining your role and your contribution to the school.

Rehearsal can extend much further than this as well, as we will discover in the next entry.

Mock Ofsted

35 A mock Ofsted is exactly that – a rehearsal in preparation for the real thing. In some areas, the local authority will provide a service you can request or buy in. It is also possible to pay external companies or consultants to do this. Finally, you might do an internal mock Ofsted using the Ofsted guidance and the expertise of senior leaders.

The advantage of getting people from outside the school to do your mock Ofsted is that they will be able to offer a different perspective; one that is hopefully objective and honest.

If you do choose to do a mock Ofsted, it is important to think about the impact this will have on your staff. The best approach is to manage the process so as to make it completely non-threatening and clearly tied to the school's desire to improve.

Communicate to Colleagues

36 Good communication is at the heart of good leadership.

Great communication is the essence of great leadership.

If you are preparing for an inspection, so too are your colleagues – all those people who you lead. Think about how you want to communicate to them. Think in terms of their interests and their motivations. Help them, support them, teach them.

Communicating in this way will make their lives easier. This, in turn, means they are more likely to be successful.

Two dangers are out there, both of which you must guard against.

1. Ambiguity and lack of clarity. This will make it harder (sometimes impossible) for those you lead to achieve what you would like them to achieve.

2. Over-complication and excessive information. This will put people off and lead to your messages being diluted or even ignored.

Identify who you need to support and support them

37 We have been stressing the leader's role in supporting, helping and teaching those they lead. Evidence of these aspects of great leadership abounds. Look at managers and coaches in sport who are successful – they develop the people they work with.

The same is true in organisations. If a school produces a disproportionate number of leaders who go on to become head teachers, that is no accident. That school, and those people within it, made it their business to develop their staff; to train them and to teach them.

As a leader, identify who in your team(s) needs support and then give it to them. This will help you to prepare for an inspection. It will also help you and your team in and of itself.

Share Your Expertise

38 As a leader you have expertise. This expertise may be focussed on the particular area of the school for which you are responsible, on the whole school if you are a deputy or head teacher, or it may cover a number of different areas.

Wherever your expertise lies, share those parts of it which are relevant to other people, those bits which will help them. Don't wait for people to come to you. They probably won't. Not for any negative reasons, but just because they don't have the time, didn't think about it or felt it might be an imposition. Take the initiative yourself.

Share any Knowledge you Accrue

39 In terms of the wider inspection process, share the knowledge you accrue during your preparations.

For example, if you follow the advice in entries twenty-two and twenty-three and look at the documentation on the Ofsted website, including the good practice guides, share what you find out.

Similarly, if you develop a clarified and refined summary of the school's priorities and the specific things which are being done to meet these, share it. Everyone will benefit as a result. In turn, the school will be better prepared for the inspection.

Let people know clearly and explicitly what is required of them

40 In any job, people perform better if they know what is expected of them. It is exactly the same as teaching – if your students know what you expect from them, they have a far better chance of being successful.

It is easy to communicate clearly and explicitly to your team what is expected of them.

The important thing is to clarify matters in your own mind first, refine this information and then present it in a form which is simple, clear and easy to follow. If you send an extended email or begin talking without have thought about the matter first, your message will be lost and the efficacy of what you are doing will drop considerably.

So, identify what is expected of your team, both generally and specifically in terms of the inspection, and then communicate this.

And don't forget to keep repeating and teaching these messages.

Make sure people look after themselves

41 Inspections at present come without notice. The preparation period can thus be a lengthy one, with no seeming end to it. During this time, your staff will be working hard. Sometimes too hard.

Working oneself to a standstill is not a good way to prepare. This is because the quality of one's work will suffer, particularly in the classroom, where energy is always needed.

As a leader, you should take it upon yourself to make sure the people in your team, and in the school more widely, are looking after themselves.

You can do this in numerous ways. Two of the best are making your expectations clear, precise and achievable and providing people with help, support and resources which make their lives easier.

Don't Let it Become a Behemoth

42 Because if it does, stress levels will increase and everyone will get fed up!

Ultimately, if you are doing everything necessary to prepare, a lot of which involves implementing and sustaining best practice in the school (which hopefully you have done and are doing anyway), then you are doing your best. Furthermore, you can only control what you can control. And you have no control over the date or time of the inspection.

So, even if it seems difficult, try not to let the expected or impending nature of the inspection become an issue; everyone will benefit as a result.

Analyse Your School in Accordance with the Reporting System

43 We noted in entry twenty-four that, at present (April 2014), the five judgements Ofsted make are:

- Overall Effectiveness

- Achievement of Pupils

- Quality of Teaching

- Behaviour and Safety of Pupils

- Leadership and Management

You can use this as a framework to analyse your school before the inspectors come in.

The great benefit of this is that it allows you to break down what might at first seem a huge, impermeable mass (how are we doing? What is happening across the school?) into separate, smaller sections, each of which is more manageable.

This is the benefit of analysis more generally. It allows us to break something up and deal with each part in turn, thus letting us simply and effectively respond to the wider picture.

Identify Areas for Immediate Intervention

44 Having used the method of analysis suggested in the last entry, you are now in a position to identify areas which require immediate intervention.

As you will note, the process of breaking up the analysis of the school's present position has made it easier to state where any issues lie. If this has been done, you can move on to dealing with those issues.

Just to reinforce the point, consider the opposite. If you try to analyse the school as a single, giant whole, you are likely to miss things. In addition, the process will probably feel overwhelming. This is in part because there will be too much information for you to deal with in one go.

Effective analysis making use of the inspection framework is thus a straightforward path to identifying areas in which intervention is required.

Find Positive Solutions

45 Positive solutions are always better than negative solutions. This is because they look to the future and aim to secure improvements based on changing and improving things. Negative solutions tend to involve sanctions, reactive behaviour and the expression of emotions in the place of reason and critical disinterest.

For this reason, negative solutions often fail beyond the short-term.

Tips for finding positive solutions include:

- Identifying strengths within the school which can be called on to improve underperforming areas.

- Identifying strengths within the staff body which can be called on to improve underperforming areas.

- Identifying strengths within yourself which you can use to support, teach and develop others.

- Finding what already works in other schools and applying this in your own context (i.e. don't obsess over re-inventing the wheel).

- Identifying the desired outcome and working backwards from this. The desired outcome is usually outstanding progress for all pupils. This is something on which all staff can agree, making it easier to secure support for interventions and solutions.

Avoid Blame and Recrimination

46 If you find that something has gone wrong in school it is natural to feel negative emotions. These can easily lead to a desire to apportion blame and dole out accusations.

The question you need to ask yourself is: To what end?

If the end is an alleviation of your negative feelings (which it often is) then stop. Your job is to be a leader. Your job is to secure the very best outcomes for all pupils in the school. Your job is to facilitate a superb learning environment in which every student makes superb progress.

And what will you add to this if you focus on blame and recrimination? Nothing.

Instead of doing that, focus on making the positive changes which will have an impact.

(Of course, I am not advocating not holding people to account, far from it. But there is a significant difference between that and falling prey to the desire to blame and accuse.)

Evaluate the Strengths and Weaknesses of the School

47 Before the inspection team come in, evaluate the strengths and weaknesses of your school. This will serve a number of ends:

- It will allow you to talk knowledgeably and openly about what you do well and what you are trying to improve.

- It will provide the information you need to put interventions in place and to seek to develop the school's performance.

- It will show that you are proactively reflective and that you are focussed on continually trying to improve.

- It will give you an opportunity to develop a narrative which tells the story of your school – where you are, where you've been and where you're going.

- It will give you a sense of what to expect from the inspection itself, lessening the chance of surprises.

Be Ready to Play Up the Strengths

48 When you have a clear sense of your strengths, you are in a position to play these up. And don't be afraid to do so!

Obviously you do not want to appear aggressive or over-the-top in what you do (and, more importantly, you must not appear blind to your weaknesses) but the strengths of your school are just that – strengths! So talk about them.

Be ready to explain the weaknesses and how you are responding

49 Because it looks much better if you know where you need to improve and can already demonstrate what you are doing to make these improvements.

This is true of any time you are being assessed in any walk of life.

Such an approach demonstrates self-awareness, proactive thinking and intellectual maturity.

Show Pride in the Things You Do Really Well

50 We conclude our tour of 50 quick and easy ways leaders can prepare for Ofsted by remembering that, in any school, there are lots of good things happening. Showing pride in these is important – not just for the benefit of the inspection team but also for yourself, your students and your colleagues.

Celebrate and feel good about the great things that go on. Be critically aware of the weaknesses and find positive ways to eliminate these. Keep focussed on pupil outcomes. Remain good humoured, analytical and focussed in what you do. And most of all, lead. After all, that's what your there for.

There's just one thing left for me to say.

If you do get inspected, good luck!

A Brief Request

If you have found this book useful I would be delighted if you could leave a review on Amazon to let others know.

If you have any thoughts or comments, or if you have an idea for a new book in the series you would like me to write, please don't hesitate to get in touch at mike@mikegershon.com.

Finally, don't forget that you can download all my teaching and learning resources for **FREE** at www.mikegershon.com.

Printed in Great Britain
by Amazon